Fabergé and His Contemporaries

HENRY HAWLEY

Fabergé and His Contemporaries

*The India Early Minshall Collection
of The Cleveland Museum of Art*

Published by The Cleveland Museum of Art

Color plates on pages 25, 37, 115, and 119 appear in *The Art of Carl Fabergé*
by A. Kenneth Snowman and are reprinted here with the kind permission
of the publishers, Faber and Faber Ltd.

Contents

Introduction

The work of the famous Russian jeweler and goldsmith, Carl Fabergé, can be examined from several points of view. Of these the most suitable for objective analysis is the technical. Even a limited study of the products of Fabergé's workshop indicates that technically they are unsurpassed in the history of the European manufacture of objects in precious metals with enamel and jeweled decorations and hard stone carvings. Their only serious rivals are several Parisian and a handful of German workshops of the eighteenth century, and in at least one respect, the use of transparent enamels, Fabergé clearly exceeded all previous efforts. Thus it can be safely stated that the outstanding products of Carl Fabergé are technically the very best things of their kind ever to have been made in the West.

Fabergé's work is also significant from a historical point of view. In retrospect, his work seems so indissolubly linked with the last years of the Russian monarchy that it appears almost inevitable that it should have been produced in that time and place. But there is evidence to the contrary. Fabergé inherited from his father a large and prosperous jewelry concern. Had he chosen to do so, he could have undoubtedly continued the firm's traditional activities with perhaps greater financial gain than he actually enjoyed, but without the artistic success which has made his name famous. He decided, however, to begin manufacturing articles of fantasy and utility which, though made of precious materials, emphasized craftsmanship rather than mere display. This decision was made without extraneous persuasion. Fabergé created a demand for the product which he had decided to make. Therefore, his work was not, strictly speaking, determined by the society for which it was produced. On the other hand, it is likely that nowhere else in the Europe of his day was there a segment of society sufficiently large, rich, and aristocratic to support a workshop of the scale of his. Thus, in a broader sense, it is reasonable to see in Fabergé's work primary evidence about the society of the last years of the Russian empire. More specifically, Fabergé held an official appointment to the Russian court, and in works produced for them much can be learned about the tastes and interests of some of the most significant personages of his day. From a historical point of view, Fabergé's work is a fascinating phenomenon.

It is when the mid-twentieth-century man examines from the point of view of aesthetics the products of Fabergé's workshop that he may encounter some difficulty. In terms of pure design, Fabergé maintained extraordinarily high standards in the use of appropriate mater-

1

ials, in color relationships, and in maintaining a correct scale for his objects. But in reviewing a large number of his works, one finds, here and there, an object which, at first glance, one rejects on grounds of excessive imitation of nature in unnatural materials, too close copying of works of art of the past, or sentimentality of subject matter. Introspective analysis reveals that in almost every case it is the subject, broadly speaking, of the object, rather than its form, to which exception has been taken. It seems likely that as we move further away in time from Fabergé's work our negative reactions to some of his subjects may be reduced through the soothing medium of historical perspective. In the meantime, we may derive unimpeded pleasure from the great bulk of his products in which carefully conceived forms and the highest standards of craftsmanship are combined with often delightful and surprising subjects to produce objects of undeniable charm and beauty.

It was a historic point of view which initially brought Fabergé's work to the attention of India Early Minshall. She is an example of an unfortunately increasingly rare species, the intellectual hobbyist. An intense interest in Russian imperial history resulted first in her building a distinguished library of books on that subject. Unfortunately the library was largely destroyed in a fire some years ago. Next, she began to collect Fabergé's work, an activity which she pursued avidly for a number of years. And finally she undertook to learn the Russian language, a task which few have attempted without the encouragement of impelling professional requirements.

If it was an interest in Russian imperial history which first led Mrs. Minshall to collect Fabergé's work, her collection clearly demonstrates that she must very quickly have realized, perhaps intuitively, the significance of the technical and aesthetic aspects of her chosen field. It is the remarkable degree of concurrence of historic importance, technical quality, and beauty of the particular objects which makes her Fabergé collection a distinguished one. Though not of enormous size, Mrs. Minshall's collection includes representative examples of exceptionally high quality of every significant variety of object which Fabergé made—gold, enameled, and jeweled pieces of utility and fantasy, hard stone carvings, and silver and gold objects of utility. Occupying a central position in the collection are two Easter eggs. It is in this category of objects that Fabergé achieved his greatest successes. One of Mrs. Minshall's eggs is the Red Cross Egg which was presented by Czar Nicholas II to his wife Alexandra Feodorovna in 1915. Made on the eve of the disintegration of the empire and mirroring its times to perfection, it is doubtful that any object ever made by Fabergé is of greater importance historically than the Red Cross Egg. In contrast is another egg in the collection, made of lapis lazuli with its interior enameled to resemble a boiled egg, and containing as its central surprise a small crown of diamonds within which is suspended a cabochon ruby. The lapis egg, a reflection of happier times, sums up perfectly the character of Fabergé's work at its best—rich materials handled unostentatiously, beauty of design in all its parts, and an imaginative form which repeatedly delights. Little wonder, then, that Mrs. Minshall chose to collect the work of Carl Fabergé and that her collection has given so much pleasure to her and to others.

During her life India Early Minshall was consistently generous in sharing her collection both with persons who requested to view the entire collection and by lending objects from it to special exhibitions of Faberge's work. And now, by bequeathing her collection to The Cleveland Museum of Art, she has made provision for her collection to continue to be available to give pleasure, and to an even wider public than before.

A Note on the Catalogue

This catalogue has been designed to fulfill two somewhat different functions. First, for the interested person unfamiliar with Fabergé's work, a brief outline of the activities of his firm and of particular workmasters associated with it has been provided in the form of short introductions to appropriate sections of the catalogue. Second, for individuals who are specifically interested in Fabergé, as full and accurate information as possible has been included about the objects which comprise this collection. In some cases this has necessitated rather lengthy catalogue entries. In other cases, where little is known about the object under discussion, the entries are quite short. When information on such matters as condition or provenance is not included in an entry, the reader may presume that to the cataloguer's knowledge no relevant material exists.

In the writing of this catalogue, every effort has been made to distinguish between fact and opinion. Since much of the information currently available on Fabergé's activities is based not on published documents but on an oral tradition supplied by former associates of the firm and Fabergé's descendants, it is possible to present very little material which can be demonstrated to be factual. However, reference to previously published sources has been indicated, enabling one at least to trace the source of traditions. Unpublished opinions, particularly those relating to provenance, have been included, but their questionable reliability has been indicated. In most cases such opinions were culled from the sometimes extensive descriptions which dealers provided for articles purchased by Mrs. Minshall. Opinions relating to the condition and technical or aesthetic quality of particular objects are those of the cataloguer, except when otherwise indicated.

The catalogue is divided broadly into two sections: first, objects made in St. Petersburg, now Leningrad; and second, those made in Moscow. Stylistic differences determined that division. The catalogue has been further divided into sections dealing with the products of the various workshops which were associated with the Fabergé firm or were independent. A few attributions have been made of unmarked objects to particular workmasters, but in most cases they have been attributed either to the Fabergé firm or to anonymous makers. The limitations of our present knowledge seemed to demand that procedure.

During the period of Fabergé's activity, the marking of gold and silver in Russia was fairly consistent and uniform, though some items in which these metals played an unimportant role went unmarked. Wares were marked with a hallmark. Before 1896 it was a crossed anchor and sceptre mark in St. Petersburg and a representation of St. George in Moscow. After that date a female head in profile, facing either right or left and wearing the traditional Russian headdress, the Kokoshnik, was used in both cities. Numerals indicating the percentage of precious metal in the article were used—56 and 72 for gold, the approximate equivalents of fourteen- and eighteen-karat gold by our standards, and 84, 88, or 91 for silver. Often the initials of the tester responsible for the assaying of the metal were also included. When they are present, the hallmark, percentage numerals, and tester's initials were usually combined into a single punch, but examples are found of the hallmark and percentage numerals in separate punches as well. Usually one or two additional marks were punched which constituted the full name or initials of the workmaster who made the object and/or the firm through which it was sold. Objects made by the Fabergé firm, and probably by other firms as well, often include additional numbers lightly scratched on the objects. These are shop order numbers, and at the present time they are of very little use in determining when, where, or by whom a particular item was made. If the records of the Fabergé firm ever become available, they may, however, be of great value. Even without those records, they may be of some help when enough items have been published, together with the scratched marks which they bear, for a pattern of their use to be apparent. At present about all that can be said is that the scratched numbers on articles made by the Fabergé firm seem usually to consist of four or five Arabic numbers, with no letters or marks of punctuation. It is always possible, however, that scratched marks may have been added by dealers through whose hands objects passed at a later time. Many dealers customarily add such marks. In this catalogue every effort has been made to record completely all of the marks which appear on the items included, even when they are at present of no value because their meaning is not known. However, because on some of the items in this catalogue the same marks are repeated many times, no attempt has been made to record the number of times a particular mark occurs on a given piece, nor the location of the marks. Foreign import marks and other marks which occur rarely have been explained in the catalogue entry of the object on which they occur. Other marks are recorded in the explanatory material which introduces the various sections of the catalogue.

BIBLIOGRAPHY

The best single source of information about the work of Carl Fabergé and his firm is Snowman's monograph. Marvin Ross's catalogue of the collection of Mrs. Post includes other valuable information, particularly on Fabergé's contemporaries, and an extensive bibliography. The following are works frequently cited in this catalogue, with the abbreviations used in those citations:

Bainbridge   Henry Charles Bainbridge, *Peter Carl Fabergé, His Life and Work* (London: B. T. Batsford, Ltd., 1949).

Ross   Marvin C. Ross, *The Art of Karl Fabergé and His Contemporaries,* . . . (Norman, Oklahoma: University of Oklahoma Press, 1965).

Snowman   A. Kenneth Snowman, *The Art of Carl Fabergé* (London: Faber and Faber Ltd., 1962).

The following are catalogues of exhibitions in which many items from the Minshall collection were included.

Victor J. Hammer, Hammer Galleries, New York, *Loan Exhibition of the Art of Peter Carl Fabergé . . . March 28, 1951-April 28, 1951* (New York, 1951).

A la Vieille Russie, Inc., New York, *The Art of Peter Carl Fabergé . . . October 25-November 7, 1961* (New York, 1961).

David Graeme Keith, ed., *Fabergé* (San Francisco: M. H. De Young Memorial Museum, 1964).

I wish to express my special thanks to Marvin C. Ross, who very kindly offered many suggestions in the preparation of this catalogue. The firm of A la Vieille Russie, Miss Jessie McNab of the Metropolitan Museum of Art, and Mme. Postnikov-Losseva of the Moscow State Historical Museum also supplied useful information. Elizabeth Ourusoff de Fernandez-Gimenez helped with the translation of some of the inscriptions and the identification of persons associated with particular objects. Margaret Marcus gave assistance, particularly with the identification of the flowers. Mary Flahive of the Natural Science Museum in Cleveland advised on the identification of the gems and hard stones.

HENRY H. HAWLEY
Associate Curator of Decorative Arts

Catalogue

Fabergé's St. Petersburg House

Fabergé's establishment in St. Petersburg was the primary source of the objects of luxury which won him an international reputation during his lifetime and have assured his continuing fame. In 1842, four years before Carl Fabergé's birth, his father, Gustav, opened a business as a goldsmith and jeweler in St. Petersburg. Though the family was French Huguenot in origin, they had probably left France in 1685, after the Revocation of the Edict of Nantes, which withdrew the toleration previously granted to Protestants. Gustav Fabergé was born in Germany. His business must have thrived in St. Petersburg. His son was given a good education, and in 1860 the elder Fabergé retired with his wife to Dresden. Carl remained in St. Petersburg, where he received excellent training as a jeweler and goldsmith from his father's old associate, Peter Hiskios Pendin. Beginning in 1861, he spent several years in Germany, England, and France, where he learned languages and business methods, as well as enjoyed a generous exposure to European art. In 1870, at the age of twenty-four, Carl Fabergé became head of the firm which his father had established. It was not, however, until more than ten years later, probably not until after 1882, when Carl's brother Agathon joined the firm, that it decisively changed its course from that of a traditional jewelry concern to the production of objects of fantasy and other luxurious goods which were distinguished by their fine craftsmanship and design, rather than the mere display of precious jewels. It was probably in 1884 that the first of the series of imperial eggs was delivered. Shortly thereafter Alexander III awarded a Royal Warrant to the Fabergé firm. A design for future greatness had been established.

The organization of Fabergé's St. Petersburg house was rather complex. There were a number of semi-autonomous workshops, each with its workmaster. Most of the workmasters entered into agreements with Fabergé to produce wares only for his firm. They remained entirely responsible for the internal administration of their shops. The various shops specialized in certain sorts of work—jewelry, hard stone carvings, gold and enamel objects of fantasy, etc. However, Fabergé not only insisted upon a high technical quality for the objects produced for his firm, but also determined their general style. In many cases Carl or Agathon Fabergé actually designed particular objects, and other designers were employed by the firm to supply the various workmasters with detailed renderings of the wares which were to be made.

This relationship between the Fabergé firm and the workmasters who supplied it is reflected in the marks which appear on its products. A number indicating the standard of the silver or gold content and the St. Petersburg hallmark—the crossed anchors and sceptre mark before 1896, the Kokoshnik mark after that date were, of course, to be found both on Fabergé's wares and those of all other St. Petersburg makers. Sometimes included in the punch with the number indicating the purity of the metal and the Kokoshnik were other marks. In the Minshall collection the following such marks occur: AP for an unknown tester; ЯЛ for the tester Jacob Liapunov, 1896-1903; a lower-case Greek alpha in script, used on objects made in St. Petersburg in the years immediately before the Revolution. Customarily, objects made of gold or silver were also marked with the workmaster's initials and the name Fabergé, usually in Cyrillic capitals (ФАБЕРЖЕ), but sometimes in Roman. The mark of the Royal Warrant, the double-headed eagle, did not customarily appear on the objects themselves, since it had been awarded to the Fabergé firm, not to the various workshops. It was, however, used to mark the boxes in which Fabergé's products were sold. Certain sorts of objects—particularly those which were largely or entirely the work of the lapidary, for example the carved animals—were usually not marked. Even works made of gold or silver were sometimes unmarked or incompletely marked. Therefore, the ultimate test for determining whether or not a particular object was made for the Fabergé firm must be its style and quality.

Perchin was born in 1862. After being apprenticed to several goldsmiths, he opened his own workshop in 1886 and immediately began his association with Fabergé which lasted until his death in 1903. Perchin's was the major workshop for the production of objects of fantasy and enameled gold wares which constitute the chief glory of Fabergé's St. Petersburg house. After his death the workshop was taken over by his chief assistant, Henrik Wigström. Perchin's mark was MΠ.

The teapot and cover were carved from light green jade. They are mounted in gold in the rococo style. H. 2-1/4″; W. 4-1/4″; Diam. 2-1/16″. Marks: 56, crossed anchors; MΠ; ФАБЕРЖЕ; 47274 scratched. Made before 1896.

Exhibited: New York, A la Vieille Russie, 1961, p. 82, no. 275; San Francisco, De Young Museum, 1964, p. 58, no. 131.

Products of the Fabergé firm in the rococo style seem to have been made at a comparatively early date, before 1903, when Perchin headed the most important of the workshops.

2. Miniature Shoe. 66.482

The shoe was carved of bloodstone or heliotrope and mounted in gold in the rococo style. The buckle consists of rose-cut diamonds mounted in silver.

H. 2-13/16″; W. 3-1/2″; D. 1-5/16″. Mark: 49194 scratched. Probably made before 1903.

Exhibited: New York, A la Vieille Russie, 1961, pp. 80, 82, no. 276; San Francisco, De Young Museum, 1964, p. 32, no. 132.

The rococo style of this shoe (see preceding entry) and the high quality of its execution indicate that it was made in the Perchin workshop. The carving of the stone is said to have been executed by Kremlev.

13

3. Parrot on a Perch. 66.447

The parrot is carved of jasper and has emerald eyes.
He sits upon a ring of green enamel suspended from
a stand made of silver decorated with white enamel.
The tail feathers, now of green agate, are a recent
replacement for the original ones which were carved
from the same piece of jasper as the body of the
parrot.

H. 6″; Diam. of base 2-7/8″. Marks: 88, Kokoshnik,
tester's initials ЯЛ; МП imperfectly struck;
ФАБЕРЖЕ; 6817 scratched. Made 1896-1903.

Ex collection: Sale, Objects of Art and Virtu and
Works by Carl Fabergé, Christie, Mason, and
Woods, London, Tuesday, November 25, 1958, p.
24, no. 152.

Similar example: Parker Lesley, *Handbook of the
Lillian Thomas Pratt Collection* (Richmond: The
Virginia Museum of Fine Arts, 1960), fig. 8, no. 40,
p. 26.

The alteration of the tail feathers was carried out
after the sale at Christie's in 1958 and before Mrs.
Minshall's purchase of the object in 1960.

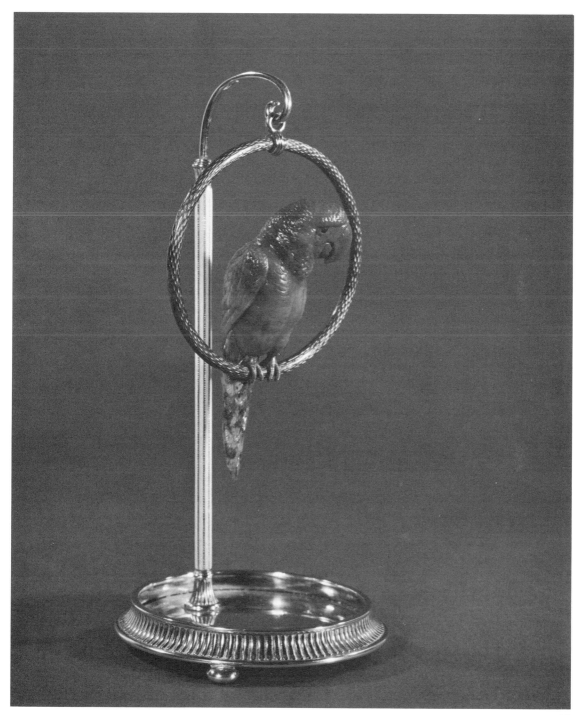

4. Compass Mounted in a Miniature Table. 66.480

The compass is seen beneath the glass top of a miniature table, which has four legs in the Louis XVI style. The table is gold, decorated with a border of laurel leaves against a blue enameled ground.

H. 2-3/16″; Diam. 1-5/8″. Marks: 56, crossed anchors; МП; ФАБЕРЖЕ. Made before 1896.

Exhibited: New York, Hammer Galleries, 1951, p. 13, no. 52; New York, A la Vieille Russie, 1961, p. 83, no. 277; San Francisco, De Young Museum, 1964, pp. 40, 41, no. 98.

5. Cup. 66.483

A fluted gold cup is decorated with alternating rose-cut diamonds and cabochon sapphires. Applied opposite the handle is a double-headed eagle in rose-cut diamonds with the arms of Russia in gold superimposed upon it. A cabochon sapphire is set into the handle.

H. 1-11/16″; W. 3-1/8″; Diam. 1-13/16″. Marks: 56, crossed anchors; МП; ФАБЕРЖЕ; 40139 scratched. Made before 1896.

Provenance: Said to come from the Alexander Palace. Exhibited: New York, Hammer Galleries, 1951, p. 14, no. 69.

19

6. Swivel Seal. 66.488

Into a small rectangular slab of yellow stone or glass are cut facsimiles of the signatures "Micha" in Roman script on one side and "Mikhail" in Cyrillic script on the other. The seal is mounted in a swivel of two-colored gold with a ring for suspension.

H. 1-11/16"; W. 1-3/8"; D. 1/4". Marks: 56; crossed anchors; МП; ФАБЕРЖЕ; 59818 scratched. Made before 1896.

Similar examples: Snowman, pl. XXXII; Ross, p. 44.

7. Lady-bug Box. 66.465

A small, hinged gold box in the form of a lady-bug. On the bottom of the box, the legs of the insect are executed in gold. The back of the lady-bug is decorated with red, black, and white enamel and rose-cut diamonds. The red enamel in the area of the hinge appears to have been damaged and repaired.

H. 13/16″; W. 1-15/16″; D. 1-3/8″. Marks: 56, Kokoshnik; МП; ФАБЕРЖЕ. Made 1896-1903.

Exhibited: New York, A la Vieille Russie, 1961, pp. 42, 50, no. 128; San Francisco, De Young Museum, 1964, pp. 30, 31, no. 57.

Similar example: Ross, p. 97.

8. Pair of Framed Miniatures. 66.458- 459

Miniatures of Czar Nicholas II and one of his children, probably Grand Duchess Olga, are framed in two-colored gold and supported on pyramidal plinths of pale green jade, mounted in gold and embellished with two small cabochon rubies.

H. 6″; W. 1-15/16″; D. 1-15/16″. Marks: 56, crossed anchors; МП; ФАБЕРЖЕ; 312H and BMM1 + scratched on 66.458; Bmm 1- 1- and 54471 scratched on 66.459. Inscribed: Zehngraf. Made probably in 1896.

Provenance: Said to come from the Alexander Palace, Tsarskoye Selo. Published: Snowman, pl. XVIII. Exhibited: New York, Hammer Galleries, 1951, p. 36, no. 215; New York, A la Vieille Russie, 1961, pp. 61, 63, no. 188; San Francisco, De Young Museum, 1964, p. 56, no. 114.

The frames were made not later than 1896. If the miniatures are those originally installed in the frames, and there is no reason to think they are not, then the child represented is most likely Grand Duchess Olga, the eldest of the children of Nicholas II, who was born in November 1895. She was heir presumptive to the throne until the birth of her brother, Alexis, in 1904. The child pictured in the miniature has been described as Alexis, but that seems unlikely because he was not born until almost ten years after the frames were made. The children of Nicholas II looked remarkably alike, especially when very young, which makes the identification of the child portrayed difficult on the basis of internal evidence. Zehngraf, who signed both miniatures, was a specialist in portrait miniatures who was employed by Fabergé.

9. Heart-shaped Frame. 66.457

The frame is made of gold with a ribbon of translucent pink enamel at the top. Its glass is thick and convex. Contained within the frame is a picture, apparently a tinted photograph, of one of the children of Czar Nicholas II, perhaps the Czarevitch Alexis, who was born in 1904. The present picture is probably not that originally installed in or intended for this frame, since it has been rather crudely altered in its lower extremity in order to be fitted compositionally into the unusual shape of this frame. The enamel on the ribbon at the top of the frame has been damaged.

H. 2-1/16″; W. 1-1/4″. Marks: 56, crossed anchors; МП; ФАБЕРЖЕ. Made before 1896.

Provenance: This frame is said to have come from the apartments of the Czarina Alexandra Feodorovna at Tsarskoye Selo, but this provenance seems doubtful.

If the child represented in the picture is indeed the Czarevitch, the picture could not be original to the frame since the latter was made before 1896 and the Czarevitch was born in 1904. The child pictured may possibly be one of the older children of Nicholas II, perhaps Grand Duchess Olga, who was born in 1895.

Wigström was of Swedish ancestry, but was born in Finland in 1860. From the opening of Perchin's workshop in 1886, Wigström was his chief assistant. After Perchin's death in 1903, Wigström assumed management of the workshop. He maintained the high standards set by Perchin. The workshop continued to be the most important of those associated with the Fabergé firm until its closing in 1917. Wigström's mark was H.W.

The petals of the flower are made of a mat white stone, the stamen of gold tipped with sapphires, the calyx of jade. The stem is of gold with a jade bud and two jade leaves. The pot is rock crystal. One of the leaves has been broken and reshaped.

H. 5-3/8″; Diam. of pot 1-1/2″. Marks: 72; H.W.; ФАБЕРЖЕ. Made after 1903.

Exhibited: San Francisco, De Young Museum, pp. 24, 25, no. 31.

The identification of this flower is difficult. It was formerly described as a white rose. The blossom and bud could be those of a rose, but the leaves certainly are not. It is perhaps a Russian wildflower which is not included in standard horticultural works.

11. Red Cross Egg. 63.673

This egg is made of gold and silver gilt. The exterior is decorated with white transparent enamel on an engine-turned ground. Centered on the front and back of the egg are crosses of red transparent enamel. In the center of the cross on the back is a circular portrait miniature of Grand Duchess Olga, and on the front, one of Grand Duchess Tatiana, both shown in their Red Cross uniforms. They were daughters of Nicholas II and Alexandra. The front of the egg divides into two quarters when opened, revealing within a triptych. The central scene is the Harrowing of Hell. Christ stands in the center atop the doors of Hell which he has just broken down. He grasps Adam by his right hand and he is surrounded by patriarchs and prophets. The Harrowing of Hell is the customary method of representing the Resurrection in the Orthodox church. Princess Olga, the founder of Christianity in Russia, is represented on the left wing of the triptych, the Martyr Saint Tatiana on the right. The central scene is painted in natural colors, but with a general golden tonality as tradition prescribes for its subject. The wings are decorated in natural colors on gold grounds. According to Snowman (p. 107), the interior miniatures were executed by Prachov, a miniaturist associated with Fabergé, who specialized in icons. The borders and major inscriptions are in white opaque enamel. The egg is accompanied by its original white velvet case and by a gold stand which was probably not made for it until fairly recently.

H. 3-3/8"; W. 2-1/2". Marks: 72, Kokoshnik, lower-case alpha in script; H.W.; ФАБЕРЖЕ. Inscribed (interior of egg): A θ and imperial crown for Alexandra Feodorovna; 1915; inscriptions in Cyrillic, Old Church Slavonic, and Roman letters which identify Sts. Olga and Tatiana and presumably describe the central scene of the triptych. Inscribed (on velvet case): Double-headed eagle, Fabergé, Petersburg, Moscow, London, all in Cyrillic on lining of case; 17.559, abbreviation for "Red Cross" in Cyrillic in ink on outside of case. Completed 1915.

Provenance: Presented by Nicholas II to his wife Alexandra Feodorovna on Easter, 1915. Published: Snowman, p. 107, figs. 378-381. Exhibited: New York, Hammer Galleries, 1951, pp. 27, 31, no. 162; New York, A la Vieille Russie, 1961, p. 91, no. 291; San Francisco, De Young Museum, 1964, p. 38, no. 144.

According to Snowman (p. 107), only the mounts of this egg are made of gold and its cost was held to about £200 as a wartime economy measure.

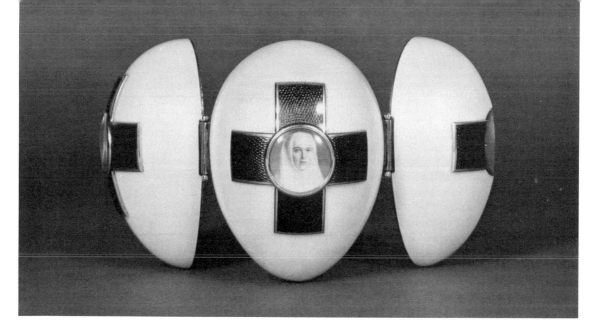

12. Miniature Bidet. 66.455

This miniature bidet in the Louis XVI style is made
of gold. The seat, made of jade, is hollowed out and
lidded. The lid and both sides of the back are decorated with sepia and opalescent transparent enamel
over an engine-turned ground, simulating the ap-
pearance of brocade. The front side of the back is
rimmed with half pearls. It has been stated that the
intended function of this miniature bidet was as a
receptacle for salt.

H. 3-1/4″; W. 1-3/8″; D. 1-3/4″. Marks: Kokoshnik,
72, lower-case alpha in script; 72; Kokoshnik; H.W.;
Fabergé; 25256 scratched. Made after 1903.

Published: Bainbridge, pl. 38; Snowman, pl. LII.
Exhibited: New York, A la Vieille Russie, 1961, pp.
79, 81, no. 272; San Francisco, De Young Museum,
1964, p. 58, no. 129.

On this chair the mark "Fabergé" is in Roman
letters rather than the more usual Cyrillic, indicating that it was intended to be sold outside of Russia,
perhaps through Fabergé's London shop.

33

13. Elephant Bell Push. 66.474

An elephant carved from an opal with ruby eyes, trappings of gold set with rubies, emeralds, and diamonds, and gold feet set with diamonds stands upon a fringed carpet of red enamel over an engine-turned gold ground with borders of diamonds, green enamel, and two cabochon rubies. The whole rests upon a plinth of light green jade.

H. 2-5/8″; W. 3″; D. 2-1/8″. Marks: 56, Kokoshnik; H. W. Made after 1903.

Provenance: Said to have been made for the Dowager Empress Maria Feodorovna, who was by birth a Danish princess. The elephant was one of the symbols of the Danish royal family.

Exhibited: New York, Hammer Galleries, 1951, p. 13, no. 57; New York, A la Vieille Russie, 1961, pp. 66, 80, no. 225; San Francisco, De Young Museum, 1964, p. 35, no. 91.

Similar examples: Ross, pp. 19-20, describes another elephant bell push and discusses other examples of elephants in Fabergé's *oeuvre*.

14. Clock. 66.475

A rectangular pillar of jade was hollowed out and provided with a mechanism to function as a clock. On the face pink enamel roses separated by green enamel leaves serve in lieu of numerals. The hands are paved with rose-cut diamonds. Four groups of three parallel bars of diamonds decorate the surface, one on each side and two on the front. These bars appear to form the Roman numeral three, and imply that the clock was designed as a third anniversary gift.

H. 3-1/16″; W. 1-5/16″; D. 15/16″. Marks: 72, Kokoshnik, lower-case alpha in script; 72; H. W.; Fabergé; 22681 scratched; NS/ 15)P scratched. Made after 1903.

Published: Snowman, p. 147, pl. XXVIII. Exhibited: New York, Hammer Galleries, 1951, Addenda, no. 332; New York, A la Vieille Russie, 1961, pp. 59, 63, no. 178; San Francisco, De Young Museum, 1964, p. 34, no. 90.

The use of Roman letters for the mark "Fabergé," rather than the customary Cyrillic, implies that this clock was made to be sold outside Russia, probably through Fabergé's London shop.

15. Clock. 66.476

This clock is made of an almost square tile of rhodenite with beveled edges. The works are encased in
silver. The dial is decorated with opalescent enamel
over an engine-turned ground and surrounded by a
border of rose-cut diamonds.

H. 2-1/16″; W. 1-15/16″; D. 1-1/8″. Marks: 88,
Kokoshnik, lower-case alpha in script; H. W.;
ФАБЕРЖЕ; 26217 scratched; swan. Inscribed:
Fabergé in script on face; an abbreviation of "week-
ly wind" engraved in Cyrillic script on back. Made
after 1903.

Provenance: Said to come from the apartments of
the Grand Duchess Tatiana in the Alexander Palace, Tsarskoye Selo. Exhibited: New York, Hammer
Galleries, 1951, p. 21, no. 137 (?).

The swan is the French import mark for silver, in
use after 1893. This clock was acquired by Mrs.
Minshall in 1937. It is the first object by Fabergé
acquired by her which can be identified with an
existing sales receipt; thus, the date of its acquisi-
tion is known.

16. Hand Seal. 66.437

An egg made of purpurine, a dark red glass made at
the Imperial Glass Factory in St. Petersburg, is
mounted in gold and raised above an oval base of
jade by gold supports which allow the egg to swivel.
Two rose-cut diamonds are mounted at the juncture
of the supports and the mounts of the egg. Almost
certainly this object was intended as a hand seal. The
bottom of the jade base was to have been carved with
a coat of arms or other design, but the carving was
never executed.

H. 1-13/16″; W. 1-9/16″; D. 1-1/4″. Marks: 56,
tester's initials AP; H. W. Made after 1903.

17. Cosmetic Box. 66.467

This box is made of silver with gold borders and silver-gilt interiors. It is divided into three compartments. The larger, central compartment has a mirror inside the cover. The box is decorated with transparent pink enamel over an engine-turned ground and borders of opaque white enamel. On the cover there is an "O" in rose-cut diamonds, and the three thumb pieces are also set with rose-cut diamonds. The pink enamel has been chipped.

H. 9/16″; W. 4-1/16″; D. 1-13/16″. Marks: 88, Kokoshnik, lower-case alpha in script; 88; H. W.; ФАБЕРЖЕ; 19838 scratched; swan; owl. Made after 1903.

Exhibited: New York, Hammer Galleries, 1951, p. 22, no. 150.

Similar example: Bainbridge, pl. 22 below.

The swan and the owl are French import marks for silver and gold, in use after 1893.

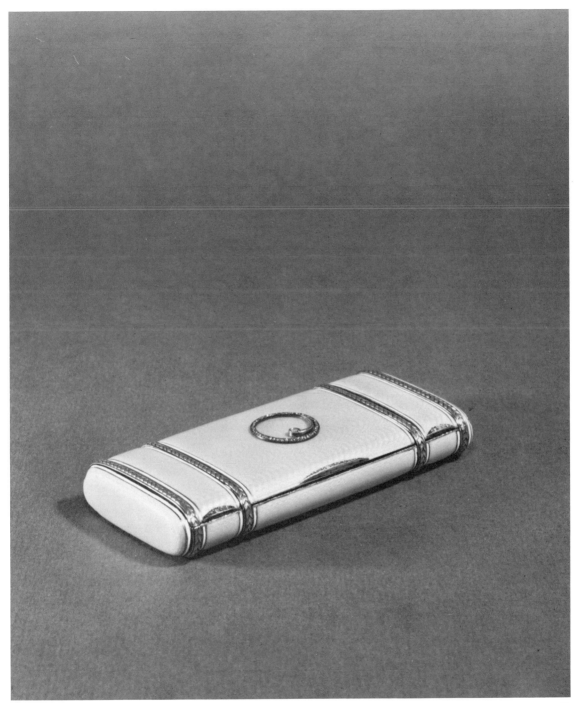

An oval miniature painting of Hampton Court near London executed in sepia and transparent opalescent enamel on an engine-turned ground is framed in jade mounted with gold decorated with white enamel. The miniature is backed with an ivory plaque.

H. 2-11/16"; W. 4-7/16". Marks: 56, Kokoshnik, lower-case alpha in script; Kokoshnik; H. W.; 19677 scratched. Inscribed: The miniature is signed at the lower right with what appears to be the Cyrillic capitals "ЯГ" in monogram. Made 1903-1910.

Ex collection: Bradshaw (bears a printed label). Published: Bainbridge, p. 98, mentions that during the reign of Edward VII (1901-1910), a miniature of Hampton Court in monochrome, framed in jade, was made by Fabergé for his London shop. Exhibited: New York, Hammer Galleries, 1951, p. 36, no. 218 (?).

Similar examples: Bainbridge, pls. 89-91; Snowman, fig. 91.

Among the miniature painters recorded as having been employed by Fabergé only one, I. Geftler, has initials which might have been represented by the Cyrillic capitals "ЯГ" His first name is unknown, but it is doubtful that the same name would be represented both by the Roman initial "I" and the Cyrillic "Я." A Mr. Bradshaw lent a number of examples of Fabergé's work to the Exhibition of Russian Art, 1 Belgrave Square, London, 1935, but this framed miniature does not seem to have been included.

Holmström was of Swedish ancestry, but was born in Helsinki, Finland, in 1829. After serving his apprenticeship in St. Petersburg, Holmström bought a workshop there in 1857 and became the chief jeweler for the Fabergé firm. After August Holmström's death in 1903 his workshop was continued by his adopted son, Albert Holmström. The mark of both August and Albert Holmström was A. H.

Four, of originally a set of six, buttons made of gold and silver which were designed to be easily adapted as pins by screwing on an attachment. They are decorated with gold transparent enamel and sprays of leaves in sepia enamel on an engine-turned ground. The borders are of rose-cut diamonds. These buttons are accompanied by their original holly wood box.

Diam. 1-3/8″. Marks: Kokoshnik; AH; 3927 scratched. Inscribed: Double-headed eagle; ФАБЕРЖЕ; St. Petersburg, Moscow in Cyrillic (inside lid of box). Made after 1896.

The other two buttons from the set are owned by Howard Greer, the California designer. Mrs. Minshall had one of the buttons adapted as a ring. This mounting has been removed. Marvin Ross (p. 86) has attempted to date Fabergé objects still in their original boxes on the basis of the names of cities in which branches of the firm were in operation at particular times. According to such evidence these buttons should have been made between 1887, the year of the opening of the Moscow branch, and 1890, when the Odessa branch opened, but the Kokoshnik with which they are marked indicates that they were made after 1896. There seems to be no reason to doubt that the box which accompanies them is their original box. Similarly the Red Cross Egg (no. 11) is dated 1915, but its original case inscribed only with the names of three cities — St. Petersburg, Moscow, and London — not Odessa, where the branch of the Fabergé firm was in operation until 1918.

20. Barometer. 66.484

Aarne was born in 1863 in Viipuri, Finland. He received his training in St. Petersburg and then returned to Finland, where he became a workmaster in 1891. In the same year he returned to St. Petersburg and became associated with Fabergé. He was working in St. Petersburg at least as late as 1913, the date of the Nicholas II Equestrian Egg which he signed. He returned at an unknown date to Viipuri, where he died. Aarne's mark was BA, or occasionally J.V.A.

The case of this barometer, in the form of the lower part of a fluted column, is made of palisander wood with silver-gilt mounts. The dial of the barometer is at the top beneath a glass cover. The finial is a cabochon garnet.

H. 5-1/2″; Diam. of base 4-7/8″. Marks: 88, Kokoshnik, tester's initials ЯЛ; ВА; ФАБЕРЖЕ. Inscribed on face: Aneroid Barometer, Storm, Rain, Variable, Clear, Very Dry, all in Cyrillic; the initials GL in monogram, presumably those of the maker of the instrument. Made 1896-1903.

21. Frame with Nine Miniatures. 66.460

This frame, made of gold and silver gilt, was almost certainly designed to exhibit an already existing collection of nine portrait miniatures of various sizes representing nineteenth-century Czars, and one Czarina. The subjects are: top row, from left to right, 1. Alexander II, 2. Alexandra Feodorovna, wife of Nicholas I, 3. Nicholas I, 4. Alexander III; bottom row, left to right, 5. Alexander III, 6. Nicholas I, 7. Alexander II, 8. Alexander III, 9. Alexander III.

H. 8-1/2″; W. 9-1/4″. Marks: 88, Kokoshnik; 56, tester's initials ЯЛ; ВА; ФАБЕРЖЕ. Inscribed: Miniatures 3 (Nicholas I), 7 (Alexander II), and 9 (Alexander III) are signed I. Goffert in Cyrillic; miniature 8 (Alexander III) signed Vegner in Cyrillic. Made 1896-1903.

Provenance: Said to have come from the apartments of the Czarina in the Alexander Palace at Tsarskoye Selo. Exhibited: New York, Hammer Galleries, 1951, p. 36, no. 214; San Francisco, De Young Museum, 1964, p. 23, no. 122.

No information appears to be available on the miniature painters Goffert and Vegner.

51

Armfelt was born in Hanko, Finland, but he was of Swedish ancestry. By 1895 he was serving an apprenticeship in St. Petersburg. According to Snowman (p. 123), Armfelt took over Aarne's workshop when the latter returned to Finland. Though this may be correct, it is likely that Armfelt was working independently earlier, since Aarne was in St. Petersburg at least until 1913 and one piece in the Minshall collection by Armfelt was probably made before 1903. Armfelt himself returned to Finland in 1916. Armfelt's mark was Я.А.

This seal is made of gold of two colors. The egg-shaped finial is made of purpurine, a glass made by the Imperial Glass Works in St. Petersburg. The vase-shaped stem is decorated with transparent blue-white enamel over an engine-turned ground. Three small rose-cut diamonds ornament the band encircling the widest point of the stem. This hand seal is accompanied by its original holly wood box.

H. 1-5/8"; Diam. 9/16". Marks: 56, tester's initials A (P?); Я (A?); 14771, 3/110-4 scratched. Inscribed: A in script on base of seal; double-headed eagle, Fabergé, St. Petersburg, Moscow, Odessa in Cyrillic inside box lid. Made 1896-1903.

Provenance: The "A" which is engraved on the base of this seal is said to be in the handwriting of the last Czarina, Alexandra Feodorovna.

The St. Petersburg tester's initials A.P. seem to occur after 1896. See no. 16. The inscription inside the lid of the box accompanying this seal indicates that it was made before the opening of Fabergé's London branch in 1903. Though the maker's mark on this seal is unclear in its entirety, it can be confidently assigned to Armfelt because he was the only workmaster associated with Fabergé of whose mark the first letter was "Я."

23. Electric Lamp in the Form of a Candlestick.
66.498

This electric lamp, made of jade with silver-gilt mounts, in the form of a candlestick in the Louis XVI style, contains provision for wiring within the central shaft and an outlet for the wire through a groove cut in the square base. When received by the Museum, this lamp had been equipped with a square metal platform at the base and a metal shaft with accommodation for two light globes, a shade, and a ball finial of jade at the top. All of these parts were obviously later additions and of much poorer quality than the original lamp. They were, therefore, removed. Originally the lamp probably had a metal cylinder painted white to simulate a candle and topped by a single electric globe.

H. 8-3/16"; W. 3-5/8". Marks: 88, Kokoshnik; Я (A?). Made after 1896.

Though only the first letter of the maker's mark can be clearly read, this lamp was probably made by Armfelt because he was the only workmaster associated with Fabergé the first letter of whose mark was "Я."

Nevalainen was born in Finland in 1858. He became an apprentice in St. Petersburg in 1876. His association with Fabergé began in 1885. Nevalainen made small articles in gold and silver in Holmström's workshop. He sometimes worked for the Moscow branch of the Fabergé firm, in which cases his personal mark appears with the usual Moscow marks. Nevalainen's mark was A.N.

This box is made of pink and yellow gold in alternating ribbed bands. The thumb piece is a cabochon sapphire. The bottom has sharp parallel ridges to provide a striking surface. A modern lighter was inserted into this box without altering its original form.

H. 1-13/16"; W. 1-5/8"; D. 1/4". Marks: 56, Kokoshnik, tester's initials A(?); A.N. Made after 1896.

25. Frame. 66.462

The square silver frame is ornamented with yellow transparent enamel over a radiating engine-turned design. The photograph presently installed in the frame is of the last Czarina, Alexandra Feodorovna, aboard a yacht.

H. 4-1/2″; W. 4-1/2″. Marks: 88, Kokoshnik, tester's initials (Я?) Л; 88; A.N.; К. ФАБЕРЖЕ; 9061 or 1906 scratched. Made 1896-1903.

Provenance: Said to come from the study of Czar Nicholas II in the Alexander Palace at Tsarskoye Selo.

The mark К. ФАБЕРЖЕ indicates that this frame was sold through the Moscow branch of the Fabergé firm. The tester's initials are those of the St. Petersburg tester, Jacob Liapunov, between 1896 and 1903.

JULIUS ALEXANDROVITCH RAPPOPORT

Rappoport was born in Germany and received his training in Berlin. He settled in St. Petersburg in 1883 and established a workshop for the manufacture of silver ware. Rappoport became Fabergé's chief silversmith. He died in 1916. Rappoport's mark was I.P.

This pair of candelabra is made of silver in the Louis XVI style. The bobeches are separate, and the candelabra are made in a fashion which permits them to be easily dismantled. These candelabra are accompanied by their original box of oak. One bobeche may have been replaced at a slightly later date.

H. 11-3/16″; W. 9-7/8″; D. 4-11/16″. Marks: 88, crossed anchors; 84, crossed anchors; crossed anchors; I.P.; ФАБЕРЖЕ; double-headed eagle; weevil(?). Inscribed: Double-headed eagle, K. Fabergé, St. Petersburg, Moscow in Cyrillic (inside lid of box). Made 1887-1890.

Similar example: Snowman (fig. 35) illustrates an original drawing, which came from the Fabergé firm, for a candelabrum similar in style and form to the present examples.

The inscription inside the lid of the original box indicates that these candelabra were made after 1887, when the Moscow branch of the firm opened, and before 1890, when the Odessa branch opened. However, see under no. 19 for the limited reliability of such dating. These candelabra may have been made as late as 1896. One bobeche is marked with the double-headed eagle, a most unusual occurrence with works made for Fabergé's St. Petersburg firm. This bobeche also differs slightly in profile from the others on these candelabra, and may have been made later than the candelabra as a replacement for a lost or damaged bobeche. Rappoport occasionally worked for the Moscow branch of the firm, and when he did so, the double-headed eagle mark was included on his work. In this case, however, the marks on the bobeche are entirely typical of those used in St. Petersburg, except for the double-headed eagle. On each candelabrum there is a small rectangular punch which is probably a weevil, a French import mark for silver, in use after 1893.

The workmaster whose initials were ЕП seems
not to have been previously recorded in the
literature about Fabergé and his contemporaries.
In the Minshall collection there is a blue
enamel cigarette box which is marked ЕП
and ФАБЕРЖЕ. The marks, which are
struck close together, seem to be original and
genuine. Also in the Minshall collection, but
not included in the bequest to The Cleveland
Museum of Art, was a small picture frame in
silver and blue enamel marked ЕП, but not
ФАБЕРЖЕ. Both of these objects are of a
technical quality lower than that of Fabergé's
usual production. The best explanation of the
evidence presently available seems to be that
ЕП was a St. Petersburg maker active around
1900 whose products reflected the style of the
Fabergé firm and whose work was sometimes
sold by Fabergé. It is doubtful, however, that
ЕП had any continuous or long-standing
relationship with the Fabergé firm, as did the
recorded workmasters.

This box is made of silver gilt with blue transparent
enamel over an engine-turned ground. It has a
moonstone thumbstone set in gold.
H. 3/4″; W. 3-3/4″; D. 2-3/8″. Marks: 88, Kokoshnik, tester's initials ЯЛ; 88; ЕП; ФАБЕРЖЕ.
Made 1896-1903.

WORKS ATTRIBUTED
TO FABERGÉ'S
ST. PETERSBURG HOUSE

28. Three Puppies on a Mat. 66.451

Three puppies made of varicolored agate and chalcedony are displayed sleeping on a mat of brown stone, perhaps marble.

H. 1-1/8″; W. 4-9/16″; D. 3-7/8″. Unmarked.

Exhibited: New York, Hammer Galleries, 1951, p. 13, no. 44(?); New York, A la Vieille Russie, 1961, no. 24.

These puppies are rendered with great naturalism and the materials have been cleverly utilized in their fabrication.

29. Begging Poodle. 66.448

A poodle standing on his hind legs is made of white
and yellowish-white agate with cabochon ruby eyes.
H. 2-1/2″; W. 1″; D. 7/8″. Unmarked.
The poodle is precisely and realistically rendered.

30. Bulldog. 66.450

A bulldog made of amethystine quartz with rose-cut diamond eyes is shown seated on his haunches with his tongue protruding.

H. 1-11/16″; W. 2″; D. 1-3/8″. Unmarked.

Provenance: Said to come from the collection of Grand Duchess Tatiana, daughter of Nicholas II, in the Alexander Palace, Tsarskoye Selo.

Similar example: Snowman, fig. 242.

The intention in the carving of this bulldog seems to have been humor, rather than strict realism. It is broadly, but convincingly, carved.

31. Goldfish. 66.453

This goldfish is made of topaz with rose-cut diamond eyes set in gold. All of the fins and the tail of the fish appear to have been recut. One ventral fin has been broken close to the body of the fish.

H. 1″; W. 1-5/16″; D. 5/8″. Unmarked.

This small carving has been executed with precision and exactitude of detail.

32. Lapis Lazuli Egg. 66.436

This egg is carved of lapis lazuli mounted in gold. It opens vertically, with half pearls edging the opening and thumb pieces of gold set with a cabochon ruby and a rose-cut diamond. The interior is enameled in opaque white and yellow to simulate a boiled egg. When the enameled yolk is opened, a mechanism is activated which causes a miniature replica of the crown of Catherine the Great to rise. This crown is paved with diamonds, with a cabochon ruby at its summit. The crown can be lifted out of the egg, revealing an egg-shaped, cabochon ruby suspended within it. The crown itself can be opened on two tiny hinges, permitting the ruby egg, which hangs on a short chain, to be extracted. The egg is accompanied by a gold stand. The yellow enamel yolk has been slightly chipped and the mechanism which causes the crown to rise no longer functions properly.

H. 2-5/16"; W. 1-3/4". Unmarked.

Exhibited: San Francisco, De Young Museum, 1964, p. 37, no. 147.

Similar examples: Snowman, p. 78, figs. 313-316; Snowman, p. 111, pl. LXXXII.

In general form the lapis lazuli egg most closely resembles the egg made in 1898 for Barbara Kelch (Snowman, p. 111). However, the surprise (the miniature crown) of the Minshall egg is quite different, and recalls the one originally in the egg which is considered to have been the first imperial egg, probably made in 1884 (Snowman, p. 78). A crown containing a ruby egg also formed the surprise in the first egg presented by Nicholas II to his wife in 1895 (Snowman, pp. 84-85). Because the miniature crown and the cabochon ruby egg fit perfectly into this egg as it now exists, and there is no visible evidence of alteration, it seems almost certain that the lapis lazuli egg was made for a member of the Romanoff family, though probably not for the Czarina or the Dowager Empress, since the series of eggs made for them is both comparatively well documented and complete, and both of them had presumably received eggs containing surprises similar to the one in the Minshall egg. The absence of marks on this egg is probably explained by the circumstance that, though mounted in gold, it is largely a product of the arts of the lapidary and jeweler. A number of similarly fabricated eggs by Fabergé are either unsigned or signed with only an engraved signature, not the usual goldsmith's marks (Snowman, pp. 104-105, 106, 113). In the case of the lapis lazuli egg there is no very appropriate surface upon which a signature might have been engraved. The high technical quality, the typical design, and the imperial associations of the crown which forms its surprise all indicate that this egg was almost certainly a product of Fabergé's firm.

33. Violet. 66.442

This violet has petals decorated with opaque purple enamel, a calyx of green enamel, a silver-gilt stem, jade leaves, and a brilliant-cut diamond mounted in silver in the center of the blossom. It stands in a rock-crystal pot. The enamel of one petal has been chipped and repaired.

H. 3-7/8″; Diam. of pot 1-7/16″. Marks: 52(1?) 4(1?) scratched.

Similar example: New York, A la Vieille Russie, 1961, pp. 36, 38, no. 73.

34. Cranberry. 66.446

35. Forget-me-not. 66.444

This branch of cranberry consists of berries made of chalcedony, shading from dark red to white. The stem is of gold with jade leaves. It stands in a rock-crystal pot. One leaf is missing. There may have been some rearrangements of or additions to the berries and leaves.

H. 4-1/2″; Diam. of pot 1-7/8″. Unmarked.

Exhibited: San Francisco, De Young Museum, 1964, pp. 24, 25, no. 32.

Similar examples: Bainbridge, p. 79; Snowman, pl. LXII, fig. 302.

This specimen was formerly described as a partridge berry. Similar examples have been published as flowering quince and cranberry. The cranberry and partridge berry are closely related botanically. The former name has been chosen for the title of this example because it is the more widely known.

The blossoms are composed of five round turquoises surrounding a rose-cut diamond. The stems are of silver gilt. The flowers stand in a rock-crystal pot. The smaller of the two stems perhaps once had an additional sprig.

H. 3-1/2″; Diam. of pot 1-3/16″. Mark: 8100(?) scratched.

Exhibited: San Francisco, De Young Museum, 1964, pp. 24, 25, no. 35.

Similar example: Snowman, pl. LXII.

36. Lily of the Valley. 66.443

The larger blossoms are composed of pearls which have been flattened on one side. To this area is attached a collar of silver set with rose-cut diamonds. The smaller blossoms are simply small pearls. The stem is gold and the leaves are jade. The flower stands in a rock-crystal pot. The collar of silver set with diamonds is missing from one pearl. Another large pearl is cracked.

H. 4-3/4"; Diam. of pot 1-3/16". Unmarked.

Exhibited: New York, Hammer Galleries, 1951, Addenda, no. 344; San Francisco, De Young Museum, 1964, pp. 24, 25, no. 34.

Similar examples: The lily of the valley was one of the flower motifs most frequently employed by Fabergé. Among the examples which technically resemble the present one is one of the imperial eggs (Snowman, p. 88) and an important presentation piece (Snowman, pl. LXIII).

37. Miniature Lily of the Valley. 66.445

The blossoms are simulated by small pearls attached to a gold stem. The leaves are jade, the pot is rock crystal. The leaves have recently been glued to the stem.

H. 2"; Diam. of pot 7/8". Unmarked.

Exhibited: San Francisco, De Young Museum, 1964, pp. 24, 25, no. 33.

Similar example: Snowman, pl. LXV.

38. Wild Rose. 66.440

The blossom is enameled in opaque pink, with darker pink veins, gold stamen, and a brilliant-cut diamond mounted in silver in its center. The calyx is enameled green. The stem is gold with leaves of jade. The flower stands in a rock-crystal pot. The enamel of the blossom has been chipped in one place.

H. 4"; Diam. of pot 1-3/4". Mark: 1132(?) scratched.

Similar example: Snowman, fig. 301.

39. Stamp Moistener. 66.478

This stamp moistener has been carved of jade to simulate a tomato. A jade stem tipped by a rose-cut diamond set in gold also functions as the handle of a small sable-tipped brush.

H. 2-7/16″; Diam. 2-1/16″. Unmarked.

Similar examples: Snowman, fig. 148 (a box); San Francisco, De Young Museum, 1964, no. 108.

The function of this object has been described as a gum pot, that is, a container for gum, presumably to be used for cosmetic purposes. The shape has been described as "pumpkin."

40. Domed Bell Push. 66.472

This bell push is made of silver. It is decorated with pink enamel over an engine-turned ground. The base is of bowenite, the push of colored glass(?).

H. 1-3/8″; Diam. 2-1/4″. Marks: 88; ФАБЕРЖЕ; another illegible mark.

Although this bell push is not of the highest quality technically, the mark seems entirely genuine. The style, too, is typical of Fabergé's products.

41. Turtle Bell Push. 66.473

This turtle has a shell made of pink agate and its head, feet, and tail are of gold and silver paved with rose-cut diamonds. Its eyes are rubies. An electric bell was activated by pressing down the turtle's head. One diamond is missing from its tail.

H. 1″; W. 3″; D. 2-3/8″. Mark: 7434 scratched.

Exhibited: San Francisco, De Young Museum, 1964, p. 54, no. 95.

Technically and stylistically this bell push is consistent with Fabergé's products.

This gold box has a tinder attachment with a red and blue cord and a separate match compartment. The cover is decorated with a scene of a yacht in low relief against a hammered gold ground. At the bow flies the Russian Jack, represented in red, blue, and white enamels. From the first mast and at the stern flies the Russian Ensign in blue and white enamel. The personal standard of the Romanoffs, in yellow and black enamel, flies from the second mast. At the lower right corner of the back the personal standard of the Czarevitch, the Romanoff standard superimposed upon the Russian Jack, is represented in colored enamels. Inside the lid is an engraved inscription and the double-headed eagle paved with diamonds.

H. 11/16″; W. 3-5/8″; D. 2-11/16″. Russian Marks: 56, crossed anchors; (?) Ф. English Marks: 5, 12; omega in a square; Gothic N; GS. French Mark: ET. Inscribed: In Remembrance/from Sandro/Sevastopol/1886/6 May in Cyrillic script. Dated 1886.

Provenance: Said to have been given by Grand Duke Alexander Mikhailovitch to the Czarevitch, the future Nicholas II, on his eighteenth birthday, May 6, 1886. Exhibited: San Francisco, De Young Museum, 1964, pp. 28, 29, no. 67.

The maker's mark on this box presents considerable difficulties of interpretation because it is either imperfectly struck or has been badly rubbed or damaged. The second letter is clearly the Cyrillic "Ф." The first, which is unclear, most closely resembles in its present state a Roman "R," but this letter form does not occur in the Cyrillic alphabet. It has been read both as a "B" and a "К." The initials "В.Ф." have been recorded in one place as the initials of an unknown Fabergé workmaster (New York, A la Vieille Russie, 1961, p. 96). However, it is possible that they may have been misread, since they occurred on only one piece known to the authors of that catalogue. The initials "К.Ф." constitute one of the marks of the Fabergé firm, but

they were more often used on the products of the Moscow branch, and this box was certainly made in St. Petersburg. At least four different areas of the interior of the box show evidence of severe abrasion. It seems very likely that marks were removed from these areas. In the case of at least two other items in this collection (nos. 44 and 45), the original marks appear to have been altered or erased in order to suggest that the items had been made by the Fabergé firm when, in fact, they were not. Such might also be the case with this box. On the other hand, it is very thoroughly and generously marked with English import marks—the London import mark (an omega in a square), the standard mark 5 and 12 conjoined for 12-karat or 50% gold, the date letter, a Gothic N, for 1929, and the initials GS, probably for the dealer who had it assayed in London. It is conceivable that the original marks may have been purposely erased when the English marks were applied, except for the two small Russian marks on the flange of the lid which were overlooked and thus survived. There is no indication, however, that it was customary to erase foreign marks when English import marks were applied. The high technical quality of this box, its obvious imperial associations, and the possibility that it may have been marked К.Ф. favor its attribution to the Fabergé firm, but such an attribution cannot be put forward with certainty. If this box did come from the Fabergé firm, it was probably made in the workshop of Erik August Kollin, who specialized in gold work and had been associated with Fabergé since 1870. The ET is a French import mark.

Works by Other St. Petersburg Makers

The jewelry firm of Hahn was probably second only to that of Fabergé in St. Petersburg at the end of the nineteenth and the beginning of the twentieth centuries. As is the case with Fabergé, Hahn had received a Royal Warrant and was thus permitted to add the double-headed eagle mark to his products. Hahn's most famous commission was for the diadem worn by the last Czarina, Alexandra Feodorovna, at her coronation. Hahn's mark was K. Hahn in Cyrillic.

The box is made of carved jade with gold mounts decorated in green enamel. On the cover are oval portrait miniatures of Czar Nicholas II and his wife, Alexandra Feodorovna, enframed with diamonds. At the top of each miniature is a small crown and ribbons of diamonds. Joining the two miniatures are a crown set with diamonds and rubies and a double-headed eagle of diamonds. Beneath the miniatures are sprays of oak and laurel leaves in gold set with diamonds and rubies.

H. 1-7/16"; W. 3-5/8"; D. 3-3/4". Marks: Crossed anchors; K. - - - -; double-headed eagle; illegible mark; eagle head. Made ca.1895.

Published: Armand Hammer, *The Quest of the Romanoff Treasure* (New York: The Paisley Press, 1936), p. 239, illus. opp. p. 200. Exhibited: New York, Hammer Galleries, 1951, p. 18, no. 112; San Francisco, De Young Museum, 1964, p. 52, no. 66.

The eagle's head mark is a restricted warranty mark used in France between 1847 and 1919 for objects made in that country. Thus, the box and its mounts were certainly made in France. The present box is strikingly similar in style to a jade box in the Walters Art Gallery, Baltimore, which is marked with the eagle's head; K. Hahn; and a French maker's mark, A C and a hatchet, which is thought to be the mark of Cartier in Paris. The size of the punch indicates that the mark on the Minshall box also read K. Hahn, not K. Fabergé. In addition, the box bears the St. Petersburg crossed anchor mark and the double-headed eagle immediately above the maker's mark. Seldom, if ever, were the products of Fabergé's firm in St. Petersburg marked with K. Fabergé and the double-headed eagle. Although the box was certainly made in France, it seems entirely possible that the jeweled enframement of the two miniatures on the cover was made in Russia by the Hahn firm and added to the box which they had imported from France.

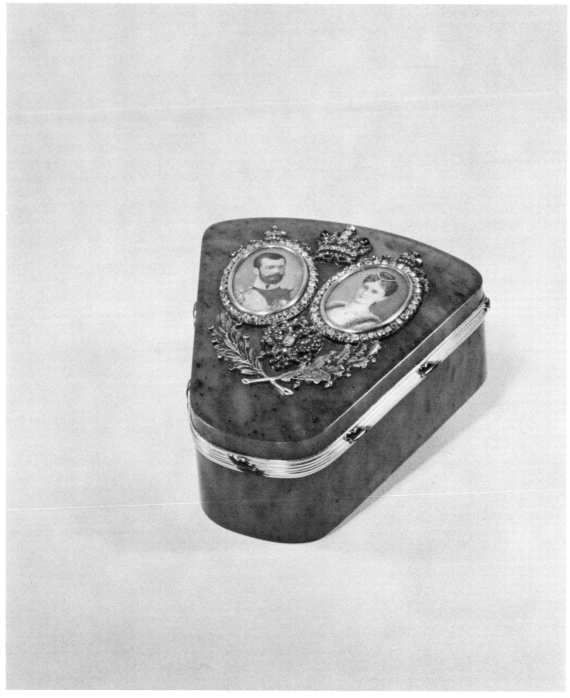

According to Snowman (p. 123), Alexander Tillander was a workmaster associated with the Hahn firm. However, L. Bäcksbacka, *St. Petersburg Jewellers, Goldsmiths and Silversmiths 1714-1870* (Helsinki: Konstsalongens Förlag, 1952), p. 247, merely lists Tillander among the St. Petersburg makers, with no mention of an association with the Hahn firm. It is possible either that Tillander did not work exclusively for the Hahn firm or that his association with it was confined to the latter part of his career. It is reported that Tillander was killed by his own workers at the outbreak of the Revolution. Tillander's mark was AT.

An egg made of gold is decorated with red enamel on an engine-turned ground. It opens horizontally with a thumb piece in the form of a cabochon sapphire mounted in gold. Engraved beneath the enamel of the top are the Cyrillic letters "XB" in monogram which signify the phrase, "Christ is risen." Within the egg, the lower half is fitted to hold the surprise, a miniature easel in gold into which is fitted a photograph of the Czarevitch Alexis, son of Nicholas II, at about eight years of age. The photograph is covered with faceted green glass and the easel is topped by an imperial crown. The inside of the top is enameled in opaque blue. The egg is accompanied by a gold stand.

H. 2-3/16″; Diam. 1-1/2″; H. of stand 1-5/8″. Marks: crossed anchors, 72; AT; S4012 ml xx scratched. Made before 1896.

Exhibited: New York, Hammer Galleries, 1951, pp. 31, 33, no. 165; San Francisco, De Young Museum, 1964, p. 37, no. 146.

The covering of the inside of the top of this egg with blue opaque enamel, though technically a sound procedure, is not typical of Fabergé's methods. The initials "AT," when they appear on an object of fantasy such as this egg, are presumed to refer to Alexander Tillander, though there were at least two other contemporary St. Petersburg makers with this mark (Snowman, p. 123). The crossed anchor mark indicates that this egg was made before 1896. The Czarevitch Alexis was born in 1904 and since his photograph in the surprise shows him at about eight years of age, it could not have been made before about 1912. It seems unlikely, therefore, that this photograph or the easel with the imperial crown in which it is framed are original to the egg. The easel is fitted into the egg in a holder made of wood or cardboard, covered with worn green velvet, and glued into the lower half of the egg. Thus, it might easily have been added to the finished egg. Neither the easel nor the stand is marked.

Britzin worked for a time with Fabergé before setting up his own firm. At least by 1916 the firm was sufficiently well established to receive commissions from the imperial family (Ross, p. 92). After the Revolution Britzin is said to have transferred his establishment to Stockholm, where it continues today, with a branch in Los Angeles. The Britzin firm produced technically sound work which imitated stylistically Fabergé's products. Britzin's mark was И.Б.

A silver cigarette box of oval section is decorated with gold enamel over an engine-turned ground. The mounts are of gold and the thumb piece is a moonstone.

H. 3-5/16″; W. 2″; D. 5/8″. Marks: 916, Kokoshnik, lower-case alpha in script; 88, Kokoshnik, lower-case alpha in script; 56; 583; И.Б.; Л.Ю.Т.; P; two long rectangular punches which were probably Britzin's full name, perhaps erased so that the box could be sold as Fabergé's work. Made ca. 1916.

The "Л.Ю.Т." mark is that of the Leningrad Jewellery Brotherhood. This box was being made or had been made but not sold when the Revolution occurred. It was completed and/or sold by the Leningrad Jewellery Brotherhood (Snowman, p. 119). The "P" mark is probably that of the examiner. (Snowman, fig. 405).

The workmaster whose mark is "A.K." was perhaps the head of one of the three St. Petersburg firms listed by Snowman (p. 129) whose owner's last names began with a "K"— Khlebnikov, Köchli, or Kortmann. All three of these firms were imitators and competitors of Fabergé. Khlebnikov seems to have been the most important of them.

This cigarette box is made of roughly cast silver with a cabochon sapphire mounted in gold as a thumb piece. The interior is gilded.

H. 5/8"; W. 3-15/16"; D. 2-13/16". Marks: 84, Kokoshnik; 56, Kokoshnik; A.K. Made after 1896.

Though this box exhibits a style which recalls that of some of Fabergé's cigarette boxes, it is technically inferior to the work of his firm.

WORKS ATTRIBUTED
TO ANONYMOUS
ST. PETERSBURG MAKERS

47. Elephant. 66.452

This standing elephant is carved from an opal.
H. 11/16″; W. 7/8″; D. 3/8″. Unmarked.
Even though its small size makes a judgment difficult, this elephant seems less realistically rendered than the products of Fabergé's firm. Compare it, for example, to the elephant bell push, cat. no. 13.

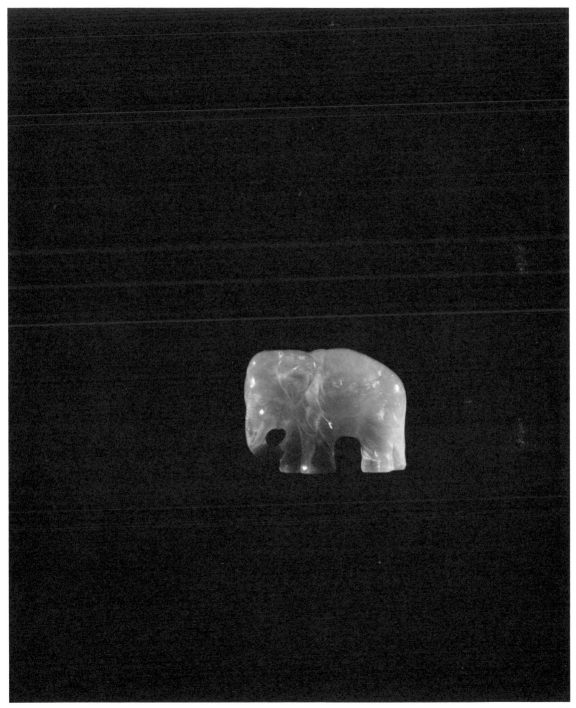

48. Rabbit. 66.449

This rabbit, sitting on his haunches, is carved of light green jade and has ruby eyes.

H. 1-5/8″; W. 2″; D. 15/16″. Unmarked.

The quality of the carving of this rabbit lacks the precision of the animal carvings produced by Fabergé's firm. It is, however, sufficiently close in style and technique to make fairly safe the presumption that it was carved in St. Petersburg during the period of Fabergé's ascendency there. Among the firms making carved stone animals there were Denissov-Duralsky and Simnov (Snowman, p. 129).

49. Hand Seal. 66.489

This gold hand seal is of a generally columnar form. At the base are two peacocks. Garlands of flowers entwine the shaft. At the top an eagle is attacking a snake. The flowers, peacocks, and snake are decorated with transparent enamels in natural colors. Beneath the base an agate is carved in intaglio with the arms of Leuchtenburg impaling the Russian imperial arms of the Romanoffs, superimposed on the double-headed eagle, and surmounted by the imperial crown. Much of the enamel decoration has been lost.

H. 2-7/8″. Unmarked. Made in 1839(?).

Provenance: The arms are those of Duke Maximilian of Leuchtenburg and Grand Duchess Marie, daughter of Nicholas I of Russia.

The present Duke of Leuchtenburg has suggested that this hand seal was presented to his great-grandparents on the occasion of their wedding in 1839. Purely on the basis of its style one would be inclined to date it slightly later, but the date of 1839 is not a stylistically impossible one. Certainly this hand seal was made earlier than the period of Fabergé's activity. The sophistication of its design and the fine quality of its craftsmanship leads one to think that it may have been made in France or Germany, rather than Russia.

50. Paper Knife. 66.486

The blade of this knife is made of agate, the collar of transparent yellow enamel on an engine-turned ground mounted in gold set with diamonds, and the ovoid finial of two pieces of rock crystal carved on their flat surfaces—one with mushrooms, the other with lilies of the valley. The intaglio carvings are naturalistically colored. The two pieces of rock crystal are joined together and bound in gold. The tip of the blade has been broken and reshaped.

H. 8″; Diam. 1-1/4″. Marks: BIMPP scratched; 017(5?) scratched. Made ca.1860(?).

Exhibited: New York, A la Vieille Russie, 1961, p. 66, no. 217.

The execution of this paper knife is technically very good. However, the decorative motifs employed— the rather relaxed rococo "C" scrolls of the collar mounting, the Gothic ogival arches included in the pattern of the engine turning, the flowers and leaves in the Louis XVI taste of the gold band at the juncture of the two pieces of rock crystal, and the simple naturalism of the intaglio carvings—suggest an earlier, less historically rigorous taste than that which inspired Fabergé's designs. Marvin Ross has suggested orally that this paper knife may have been made by the St. Petersburg firm of Nicholas and Plinke, which was active from about 1815 to the 1870's and made articles of luxury for the court.

51. Octagonal Frame. 66.499

Within the silver frame is a circular photograph of
Grand Duke Sergius, uncle of Nicholas II, and his
wife, Grand Duchess Elizabeth, who was a sister of
the last Czarina, Alexandra Feodorovna. At the top
of the frame is an enamel representing St. George
in natural colors on a red ground. The frame is accompanied by its original box of oak. An indentation
in the lining of the box indicates that a finial, probably a double-headed eagle, once rose above the
enameled St. George. At the top of the frame there
is a slot into which such a finial might have been
inserted.

H. 7″. Marks: 84, Kokoshnik, tester's initials ЯЛ;
maker's mark(?) illegible. Inscribed: Sergei in
Cyrillic with an imperial crown; Elisabeta in Cyrillic
with an imperial crown; 1891-1904; C. 1525Б in
ink on back. Made 1903-1904.

The initials ЯЛ are those of the St. Petersburg
tester, Jacob Liapunov, in use between 1896 and
1903. This frame was undoubtedly a presentation
piece commemorating an anniversary or the passage
of some definite period of time. It was not a wedding
anniversary, however, since the couple had been
married in 1884, and the frame is marked 1891-
1904.

1891 – 1904.

Fabergé's Moscow Branch

The Moscow branch of the Fabergé firm was opened in 1887 and remained active until the firm itself closed in 1918. The organization of the Moscow branch was quite different from that prevailing in St. Petersburg. In Moscow there were no semi-autonomous workshops associated with the Fabergé firm. All activities of the Moscow branch were directly controlled by the firm's management, though a division of labor into shops for silver, jewelry, and objects of fantasy was maintained. Occasionally articles made by workmasters associated with the St. Petersburg house or by independent Moscow shops were made for and sold through the Moscow branch, but this was a relatively rare practice.

The styles and techniques employed by the Moscow branch also differed, to a degree, from those of the St. Petersburg house. In Moscow opaque enamels were used in designs and on forms derived from the traditional Russian practice of this art. Such inspiration seldom prevailed in St. Petersburg. Articles which reflect a Western European tradition in style and technique were produced in Moscow as well as in St. Petersburg, but there was a subtle tendency at the Moscow branch toward more obviously opulent and less sophisticated designs than those which were customary at the St. Petersburg house. Undoubtedly these differences were in large measure dictated by the clientele served—the court circle of St. Petersburg and the rich bourgeoisie of Moscow. Technically, however, the Moscow branch maintained standards fully comparable to those of the St. Petersburg house.

The organization of the Moscow branch was reflected in the marks used there on gold and silver. The usual mark was K. Fabergé in Cyrillic (К. ФАБЕРЖЕ) with the Royal Warrant, the double-headed eagle. Fabergé's initials, К. Ф., were more frequently employed by the Moscow branch than by the St. Petersburg house. The personal marks of workmasters very seldom appeared on the wares offered by the Moscow branch. When they do, they are almost never the marks of persons directly associated with the Moscow branch, but rather of local or St. Petersburg workmasters who only irregularly supplied their products to that branch.

The Moscow hallmarks followed a pattern similar to those of St. Petersburg. The mark until 1896 was a representation of St. George combined with numerals indicating the standard of silver or gold, and sometimes with the initials of the tester who had assayed the metal. After 1896 the Kokoshnik was used in Moscow, as it was in St. Petersburg.

Marvin Ross, relying on information supplied by Mme. Postnikov-Losseva of the Moscow State Historical Museum, has published the dates of the periods during which the various Moscow testers' initials were in use. This information makes possible the more accurate dating of many articles made in Moscow. The following Moscow testers' initials, with their dates, occur on objects in the Minshall collection: ИЛ, 1896-1906; Д, 1906-1916.

52. Jade Egg with Stand. 66.434

An egg made of jade, mounted in gold(?) with a cabochon ruby as its finial opens horizontally to reveal
a metal nest containing three eggs of jade and purpurine. The egg is supported on a gold stand of complementary design which is embellished with three
cabochon rubies.

H. 2-3/16″; Diam. 1-1/2″; H. of stand 2-3/8″.
Marks: ET (egg), КФ (stand); illegible mark (stand).
Made after 1900(?).

Exhibited: San Francisco, De Young Museum, 1964,
p. 37, no. 145.

The mark "ET" is a French import mark. The
initials "КФ", for Carl Fabergé, were most often
employed by the Moscow branch of the firm, though
they might possibly have been used in St. Petersburg on an object as small and difficult to mark as
this stand. The stand is clearly of much finer quality
technically than the egg. The two could not have
been made in the same shop. However, since their
designs are complementary, one must have been
made to accompany the other. It is possible that the
Fabergé firm was called upon to supply a stand for
an already existing egg. It seems more likely that an
egg was made quite recently to enhance the com-
mercial value of a surviving Fabergé stand. It is
even possible that an egg and a stand were purposely separated recently, and their respective
missing parts reproduced, in order to create two
salable lots, each with at least one part genuinely
marked.

53. Pansy. 66.438

This pansy is made of gold with jade leaves. The petals are naturalistically colored in purple, yellow, and white opaque enamels. It stands in a rock-crystal pot. The enamel appears to have been repaired near the center of the blossom. The pot has been chipped and repaired.

H. 4-5/8″; Diam. of pot 1-7/8″. Marks: (К?) ФАБЕРЖЕ; double-headed eagle.

Similar example: San Francisco, De Young Museum, 1964, p. 24, no. 28.

Technically this flower exhibits some variations from the usual methods employed by the Fabergé firm in manufacturing this variety of object. The leaves appear to be a darker green because they are thicker, and they are somewhat stiffly rendered. The calyx is of gold. These variations from the norm can probably be explained by the circumstance of the flower's having been made by the Moscow branch, rather than in one of the St. Petersburg shops, the probable provenance of most surviving Fabergé flowers.

54. Miniature Chair. 66.454

This miniature chair is in a pseudo-Louis XVI style. It is made of gold and silver gilt and decorated in pale gray transparent enamel and floral sprigs in natural colors over an engine-turned ground, simulating a brocaded textile. Two cabochon rubies serve as finials for the posts of the chair, and rose-cut diamonds are set into the bow and ribbons at the crest and above each of the turned splats. A clever device permits the top of the seat to be raised slightly, then moved forward on its hinges, in order to be opened entirely without hitting the lower rail of the back. A small compartment is revealed within the seat. One jewel is missing from the center of the bow.

H. 4-1/8″; W. 2-1/16″; D. 1-7/8″. Marks: 56, Kokoshnik, tester's initials ИЛ; 84, Kokoshnik, tester's initials ИД; Kokoshnik; К. ФАБЕРЖЕ; double-headed eagle; КФ; 25196 scratched. Made 1896-1906.

Ex collection: J. P. Morgan, Sale, Part two, New York, Parke-Bernet Galleries Inc., March 22-25, 1944, p. 146, 147, no. 595. Published: Snowman, pl. LI. Exhibited: San Francisco, De Young Museum, 1964, pp. 40, 41, no. 130.

55. Lacquer Box. 66.464

A box made of red lacquered papier-mâché is mounted in gold enriched with six clusters of small diamonds. In the center of the top there is an imperial crown.

H. 11/16″; W. 5-11/16″; D. 1-15/16″. Marks: 56; КФ. Inscribed (inside cover): Factory N. Lukutine in Cyrillic script in gold; three double-headed eagles in gold. Made ca.1890.

Provenance: Said to have been made for Grand Duke Alexander.

The Lukutine factory, which was located in the province of Moscow, was famous for its papier-mâché boxes, and especially for those decorated in red lacquer, which was said to rival the best Oriental lacquers. N. Lukutine was manager of the factory until the end of the 1880's. This box was, therefore, probably made shortly after the opening of the Moscow branch of the Fabergé firm in 1887.

56. Triangular Frame. 66.456

This frame in the Louis XVI style is made of four colors of gold. At each end of each of the three poles which form its primary support a cabochon ruby is set. In the center is an oval miniature of the last Czarina, Alexandra Feodorovna, bordered with rose-cut diamonds.

H. 5-3/16″; W. 4″. Marks: 56, tester's initials ИЛ; 56; Kokoshnik; К. ФАБЕРЖЕ, double-headed eagle; КФ; 27280 scratched. Made 1896-1906.

Published: Snowman, pl. XIX. Exhibited: New York, A la Vieille Russie, 1961, p. 63, no. 189; San Francisco, De Young Museum, 1964, p. 23, no. 115.

57. Kremlin Tower Clock. 66.477

The form of this clock recalls in a general way several of the towers within the Kremlin, particularly the Toinitskaia. It is made of rhodenite. The mounts are of silver, and it is decorated with cabochon emeralds and sapphires.

H. 11-3/8″; W. 5-3/4″. Marks: 84, Kokoshnik, tester's initial Д; 91, Kokoshnik; 91; Kokoshnik; К. ФАБЕРЖЕ; double-headed eagle; 16419 (К?) scratched. Inscribed on clock works: Le Guet (the watch, in script); strike, silence, set hand work (in English). Said to have been made in 1913 to commemorate the 300th anniversary of the Romanoff dynasty. The tester's initial, in use from 1906 to 1916, agrees with this date, as do the other marks.

Published: H. C. Bainbridge, "The Workmasters of Fabergé," *The Connoisseur*, XCVI (August 1935), 87-90; Bainbridge, pl. 17.

58. Round Box. 66.466

This box is made of silver gilt. The enameled ornament is executed in opaque green, yellow-orange,
blue, and white, in part on a brownish-black ground.
In the center of the cover is a scene in naturally
colored opaque enamels of a horse-drawn sleigh, or
troika, driving through the snow. Some of the globules of enamel have been broken off. In places the
gilt has worn off the silver.

H. 11/16″; Diam. 2-1/4″. Marks: Kokoshnik(?),
tester's initial Д(?); 88; К. ФАБЕРЖЕ; double-
headed eagle; 25477 scratched. Made 1906-1916.

Similar example: Snowman, fig. 89.

The mark which includes the tester's initial is badly
struck. This box can be dated between 1906 and
1916 only if that mark has been correctly read. Ross
(p. 82) has remarked that the use of small globules
of silver, a technique to be found in this box, recalls
the work of Fedor Rückert, a Moscow maker who
sometimes worked for the Fabergé firm. However,
in the absence of Rückert's personal mark, it seems
unwise to attribute this box to him, since this technical peculiarity might well have been imitated by
others.

This tea set is comprised of eleven pieces as follows: a. teapot; b. hot water pot; c. covered sugar bowl; d. sugar basket; e. cake basket; f. cream pitcher; g. tea strainer; h. sugar sifter; i. sugar tongs; j. lemon fork; k. tea caddie. The set is made of silver gilt. The exterior surfaces are decorated in opaque cloisonné enamels, of which the dominant colors are green, blue, yellow brown, and white, on a mat gold ground. The borders are of dark blue enamel.

a. Teapot. H. 5″; W. 7″; D. 4-1/4″. Marks: 84, St. George; К. ФАБЕРЖЕ, double-headed eagle; St. George; КФ.

b. Hot Water Pot. H. 7-1/8″; W. 7-1/4″; D. 4″. Marks: 88, St. George; К. ФАБЕРЖЕ, double-headed eagle; 88; КФ.

c. Covered Sugar Bowl. H. 4-5/8″; W. 5-5/8″; D. 4-1/4″. Marks: 84, St. George; К. ФАБЕРЖЕ, double-headed eagle; St. George?; КФ; 10593 scratched.

d. Sugar Basket. H. 2-3/8″; Diam. 4-5/8″. Marks: 84, St. George; К. ФАБЕРЖЕ, double-headed eagle; 10593 scratched.

e. Cake Basket. H. 3″; W. 8-13/16″; D. 6-7/8″. Marks: 88, St. George; К. ФАБЕРЖЕ, double-headed eagle; 10593 scratched.

f. Cream Pitcher. H. 3-7/8″; W. 3-7/8″; D. 2-7/8″. Marks: 88, St. George; К. ФАБЕРЖЕ, double-headed eagle; 10593 scratched.

g. Tea Strainer. H. 6-3/4″; W. 2-5/16″. Marks: 84, (St. George?); К. ФАБЕРЖЕ, double-headed eagle; 11494 scratched.

h. Sugar Sifter. H. 6-7/8″; W. 2-1/4″. Marks: 84, (?); К. ФАБЕРЖЕ, (?).

i. Sugar Tongs. H. 5-1/4″; W. 1-5/16″. Marks: 84, (St. George?); К. ФАБЕРЖЕ, double-headed eagle; 11494 scratched.

j. Lemon Fork. H. 4-7/8″; W. 5/8″. Marks: 84, St. George; К. ФАБЕРЖЕ, double-headed eagle; 11494 scratched.

k. Tea Caddie. H. 6-3/8″; W. 4-3/8″. Marks: 88, Kokoshnik, tester's initials ИЛ; К. ФАБЕРЖЕ, double-headed eagle; 88.

With the exception of the tea caddie, this tea set was made before 1896. The tea caddie was made between 1896 and 1906.

Provenance: Said to come from the Alexander Palace, Tsarskoye Selo.

Although clearly made as a set, the marks on these pieces indicate that they were made in several groups, probably at various times. The earliest piece was presumably the teapot (a). At the same time or slightly later the hot water pot (b) was probably made. The covered sugar bowl (c), sugar basket (d), cake basket (e), and cream pitcher (f) all bear the same scratched shop order number, 10593, indicating that one shop order covered them all. Similarly, three of the four serving implements bear the shop order number 11494.

125

60. Covered Pot. 66.511

This covered pot is made of copper with brass handles.

H. 5″; W. 5-1/4″. Marks: double-headed eagle; К. ФАБЕРЖЕ. Inscribed: War in Cyrillic, 1914г. Dated 1914.

One of many utilitarian objects which were made by Fabergé as part of the war effort.

Works by Other Moscow Makers

Rückert, who was of German ancestry, established what was perhaps the most important Moscow workshop for the production of wares in the traditional Russian style of enamels. A measure of his success is that a part of his output was sold through the Fabergé firm and bore its mark, as well as Rückert's personal mark. Rückert seems to have been active from the end of the nineteenth century until the beginning of the Revolution. Rückert's mark was ФР.

The kovsh is a traditional Russian drinking vessel. This example is made of silver gilt. Its exterior is decorated with floral motifs, chiefly in blue, pink, and yellow opaque enamels, with borders of blue and green enamel. It is studded with cabochon gems, three chrysoprases and five carnelians.

H. 3-1/4″; W. 8″; D. 5″. Marks: —8, Kokoshnik, tester's initials ИЛ; —Р. Made 1896-1906.

Although the maker's mark is incomplete, the style and technique of this kovsh clearly indicate that it was made by Fedor Rückert.

62. Kovsh. 66.496

This kovsh is made of silver gilt. It is decorated with floral and leaf forms, chiefly in pink, green, and black opaque enamels on a cream-colored ground. The border is in dark green and blue enamels. It is studded with five cabochon gems—one citrine quartz, one carnelian, and three chrysoprases.

H. 3-3/8″; W. 8-1/16″; D. 5-3/16″. Marks: 88, Kokoshnik, tester's initials ИЛ; ФР; swan. Inscribed: CH in script monogram (owner's initials, on bottom). Made 1896-1906.

The swan is a French import mark, in use after 1893.

WORK ATTRIBUTED TO AN ANONYMOUS MOSCOW MAKER

63. Charka. 66.481

This small drinking vessel is made of gold and decorated with plique-à-jour enamels in red, blue, green, violet, and turquoise. In the center of the bowl a gold coin portraying Catherine II and dated 1776 is mounted. In the border fourteen cabochon sapphires are set. The enamel has been slightly damaged.

H. 2-3/16″; W. 4″; Diam. of bowl 2-3/4″. Unmarked.

This charka is of extremely high quality technically. It may have been made by the Moscow branch of the Fabergé firm. However, it is unmarked and no closely related marked examples have been discovered. Several other Moscow firms, for example Ovchinnikov, made plique-à-jour enamels of fine quality. Although its style indicates that it was made in Moscow, it is not impossible that it may have been made in St. Petersburg.

Work by an Unknown French Maker

64. Pansy. 66.439

This pansy is made of gold with jade leaves and a brilliant-cut diamond at the center of the blossom. It stands in a rock-crystal pot. The petals of the blossom are enameled with blue-violet, white, and yellow opaque enamels only on their front surfaces. The backs of the petals are gold. Small struts of gold wire, not visible from the front, are used to maintain the proper intervals between the petals. The gold stem is engraved with groups of punched marks.

H. 5-1/2″; Diam. of pot 2″. Marks: eagle's head; O(?), S, crossed arrows(?) within a lozenge-shaped(?) punch. Made before 1919.

Exhibited: New York, Hammer Galleries, 1951, p. 34, no. 197(?).

The eagle's head is a restricted warranty mark used on objects made in France between 1847 and 1919. The second mark is probably that of a French maker with the initials "OS," though it is badly struck and hence difficult to read. This pansy was certainly made in France, though perhaps to the order of and sold by a Russian dealer. Technically, it exhibits several variations from Fabergé's usual methods of making objects of this variety. The petals are enameled on only one side. Struts of gold wire are used to separate the petals. The jade leaves are stiff and not realistic in shape. The engraving of the veins of the leaves is stiff and unrealistic. The gold stem is engraved with groups of punched dots, rather than crisscrossing lines, as was Fabergé's practice.

Heterick Memorial Library
Ohio Northern University

NOV 29 '01

DUE	RETURNED	DUE	RETURNED
1.		13.	
2.		14.	
3.		15.	
4.		16.	
5.		17.	
6.		18.	
7.		19.	
8.		20.	
9.		21.	
10.		22.	
11.		23.	
12.		24.